How To Make Money In Binary Options

Disclaimer

This book is designed to provide condensed information. It is not intended to reprint all the information that is otherwise available, but instead to complement, amplify and supplement other texts. You are urged to read all the available material, learn as much as possible and tailor the information to your individual needs.

Every effort has been made to make this book as complete and as accurate as possible. However, there may be mistakes, both typographical and in content. Therefore, this text should be used only as a general guide and not as the ultimate source of information. The purpose of this book is to educate.

The author or the publisher shall have neither liability nor responsibility to any person or entity with respect to any loss or damage caused, or alleged to have been caused, directly or indirectly, by the information contained in this book.

Table of Contents

How Will This Book Help You?

Many people think that investment vehicles end with the stock market, bonds, government securities and the more recent mutual funds. To them, these are not only the safest bets but also the ones that in their minds can stand the test of their risk profiles. Many either do not know or dread the derivative market. This book is specifically designed to help you drive away this fear or informational asymmetry. The book specifically narrows down to options trading and goes deeper into how you can make money and prosper in the world of binary options trading. It will help you in understanding the various strategies that you can employ in binary options trading to beat the market average rate of return. Reading this book will sharpen your investment skills in binary trading.

5

Options: An Introduction

"Investing is an art not a science."

- Anonymous

For a long time, a misconception has been held that options trading in general are sophisticated investors' investment vehicle. Many investment authors and advisers have instilled the fear that options are complex and risky for 'small' investors. However, options trading offers unlimited opportunities to investors and are not as complex as many people think especially if you get the right information. Actually, options offer you a chance to take advantage of market movements. In this chapter, I introduce you to the world of options trading. I will start by a brief introduction of options trading so that if you do not have some background information in options trading, you can benefit from this chapter.

What are options?

Options represent financial instruments that offer the buyer the right but not the obligation to buy or sell an underlying financial asset at a specific price on or before a certain date. Just as you know, options are like any other financial securities or instruments with defined terms and conditions. Important to note is that options are not themselves assets but derive their values from other financial assets like stocks hence the name derivatives.

There are mainly two types of options; call and put. Call options give you the right but not the obligation to buy an underlying at a specific price on or before a certain date in the future. Buyers of calls have hopes that the price of the underlying asset will increase in the future and hence offer them opportunity to make gains in the market.

Put options on the other hand, offer the buyer an option but not the obligation to sell an underlying asset at a particular price within a specific period. Buyers of puts believe that prices are likely to decline in the near future.

Why options trading?

Options have been branded as some of the most risky investment ventures. However, over the past decades, participants in the options market have tremendously grown. Why would an investment vehicle thought to be so risky gain such popularity? There are several benefits that are attributed to this, but let us shift focus on the two main reasons why people use options- hedging and speculation.

1. Speculation

Speculation is better understood if thought of as betting on the price of an underlying asset. People base their beliefs of what the security price will be in the future as the market adjusts itself and make a bet on the predicted market movement. The use of options for speculation is what makes options a risky venture. You not only have to be accurate in determining the direction of the market movements but also the timing and size of such movements. If say you predict that the price of Microsoft stocks will likely rise in the next three months, you can buy call option which will enable you buy the stocks at a lower price and sell them at a higher price. If the market moves in your favour, you can make substancial gains. However, if the market movements do not favour you, you lose 100% of your investments (options price).

2. Hedging

Options can be an insurance policy for your investments. You can use options to hedge your investments against a downturn. For example, if assume you wish to take advantage of the upside of technology stocks like Microsoft, you can buy a put option and take advantage of the upside keeping the stocks safeguarded against any downturn.

*Key point/action step

Investing is all about determining the kind of investor you are and the goals you hope to achieve in investing. When investing in options, you have two main reasons for investing; to either hedge or speculate. It is important that you determine your reason for investing in order to invest wisely.

Binary Options: What you Need to Know

"Knowledge is power."

- Francis Bacon

Binary options as suggested by the term *binary* is two way kind of trade- all-or-nothing trade. It is typically a type of option where there are only two possible outcomes; you can either get 100% of your investment or nothing at all. It is yes/no trade if you decide to carry your investments to expiration. Nothing in the middle. I know I am now scaring you but do not be scared; the good news is on its way. Binary options allow you to trade off various possible outcomes with a relatively small capital at minimum risks.

How binary options work

Binary trading is not complex as many put it. Binary options are only 6 years old after getting the legal backing in the USA in 2008 but are quickly becoming the darling of many investors.

The process starts by you selecting an asset and predicting its price movements.

For instance assume you predict that the price of gold will be $1248 by 2PM the next day at NADEX (North American Derivative Exchange). You will buy an option that will pay off if the price of gold the next day exceeds $1248 by 2pm the next day. Alternatively, if in your own evaluation, think that the price of gold will not exceed the $1248, you will sell a binary option. Note that you are not buying a future contract on gold. You are simply betting on the price of the gold.

The price of the binary trade will depend on the future price of the asset in relation to the strike price and time to expiration. Binary options price fluctuates between $0 and $100. A binary price approaching $100 means that the buyers predictions could be true and represents a low probability for the seller. A binary price approaching zero means high probability for the seller and a low probability for the buyer. If you think that there is a 30% chance that the price of gold would exceed a $1248, you could buy a binary price at $30 and the person on the other end of the trade will pay $70 for the binary trade suggesting a 60% chance that the price of gold will not exceed the $1248 mark. In this engagement, your maximum profit is $60 and the maximum loss is $40. The opposite is also true for the person on the other end. That is how, perhaps one of the newest in vestment vehicle, works. Pretty easy to understand, isn't it?

Binary options contrasted with other options

At a glance, binary options and traditional options seem to share a lot in common. Some think that there is a fine line between the two classes of investments such that they can almost be classified under one class. Both binary and traditional options are financial derivatives deriving their value from other financial instruments. Also both instruments use similar terminologies like strike price, expiration dates and so on.

However, binary options are exotic options that exhibit different features from other ordinary options. Often-misunderstood, binary options have different structures, payoffs and many other things.

First, other options represent real financial products. They give you the right to exercise your option regarding the underlying financial product within the specified term. However, binary options are virtual products whose returns are only realized at the expiration of the term with no right to purchase the underlying financial asset.

Normal options are basically traded at the securities exchange like say the NYSE. In binary options, traders have no access to the options market. They basically trade via their brokers. There is no one binary options exchange market but very many small markets created by individual brokers.

The most conspicuous difference is perhaps the number of outcomes that accompany these classes of investments. For normal options, the outcome varies with the magnitude of price movements. For binary options, the outcome is fixed no matter the magnitude of these movements.

Benefits of binary options over ordinary options

There are significant differences between binary options and the traditional options. Just why would an investor prefer binary options to other options? Below are the reasons:

1. Binary options are simpler to trade. You do not need to understand the magnitude and timing of the price movement. All you need is to know the direction of that price movement and you will profit.

2. The time to expiration of a binary option is usually shorter. While with ordinary options, this time can be months and so on with the possibility of the market experiencing numerous changes, binary options only take a few weeks, hours, days or even minutes to mature.

3. You need less capital to trade in binary stocks. As opposed to ordinary stocks, you need less capital to venture into binary options trading. With about $25, you are good to go.

4. Binary markets are quite competitive. As such, brokers do all they can to win customers including offering you bonuses that can add up your profits. This is not so with traditional options.

*Key point/action step

The only way that you can succeed in binary trading is with the adequate knowledge about binary options as well as how these options compare with other options. While I may have provided adequate knowledge about binary options, you can never know too much; hence, you need to gather more information about binary options so that you can know all there is about binary options trading.

Types of Binary Options

"Information can bring you choices and choices bring power - educate yourself about your options and choices. Never remain in the dark of ignorance."

- Joy Page

There are many types of binary options available to you as an investor. Interestingly, the most common types of binary options not only confuse new traders but also experienced ones. I will go slow just to ensure that you get this information clear.

1. Digital binary options

Under this, we have call/put and up/down options.

Call options: You place a call option if you believe that the price will rise above the entry price.

Put options: You use this if you believe that the price will not rise above the entry price.

With up/down options, you only need to predict the direction of the price movements when you entered the market. Will it move *up/down?*

2. Touch binary options

These types of binary options come with predefined rates needed to win the trade as opposed to the trade participant just predicting the direction of the price movement. Here, you predict a level of decrease or increase it will reach (touch) and the level it will not reach (no touch). Please note that these types of binary options only trade when the market is closed, mostly during weekends. If the market touches or passes the specific level by 1700GMT on Monday, you get your returns. No touch pays when the level defined is not reached.

3. 60 seconds option

Are you the type that gets excited by quick rewards? Perhaps this is your best bet. This option expires in 60 seconds. With this, it is easy to predict the price movements. Basically, I usually recommend this option for traders who wish to profit quickly from a trending market.

4. Boundary options

This is sometimes also called range options. It differs from digital options in that two levels-upper and lower are defined. The asset must stay inside this boundary for a trader to receive any payout. This method is ideal for stable markets when trading inside the boundaries and volatile markets when trading outside the defined boundaries.

*Key point/action step

As you have seen in this chapter, there are different types of binary options that you can invest in; hence, it is important to choose wisely. My advice would be to start small with binary options that are easy for instance the boundary options that give you more leeway when it comes to anticipating price movements. However, it is up to you to choose the most suitable option to trade in depending on the returns you are looking for. If you are the adrenaline junkie kind of investor, then the 60-second option is most suitable for you.

Strategies To Employ In Binary Options Trading

"An investment in knowledge pays the interest."

- Benjamin Franklin

You too can make money in the world of binary options trading...

To this end, many shy away from venturing into this financial investment vehicle if the recent remarks by Forbes warning investors to keep off these investments options are anything to go by. The world is, however, yet to see a risk free investment option. Everybody knows that the higher the risk, the higher the returns. By employing the best strategies, binary options can offer you unlimited gains. You only need to stop living in ignorance concerning binary options trading and jump into this sea of winning investments. I have outlined several strategies you can use to be successful in options trading. Evaluate the strategies outlined below and choose what works best for you.

Take advantage of the bonuses

Many options trading brokers are offering their clients bonuses to keep abreast with the ever growing competition in the market. You can optimize the use of these bonuses in the following ways:

-Hedge binary trades using these bonuses. When you sign up with two different brokers, use your cash bonus to place opposing trades with each broker so that whilst one of the trades is losing, the other will win. In this way, you will be guaranteed profit made by your bonus cash!

-Watch out for re-deposit bonuses. A number of brokers are offering their most loyal and regular clients re-deposit bonuses each time they make qualifying deposits. It is automatic therefore that the more cash you deposit, the more bonuses are credited to your account and the more chances of making a winning trade.

Using your bonuses in the best way possible can open the door of wealth making in the binary trades for you. Do not just cash the bonuses and relax. Remember Warren Buffet said that while women fake orgasms, men fake finances.

Limit the number of wins and losses

A psychological problem with most traders is that once they make many wins, they get caught up with the excitement and enthusiasm. As such, they make imprudent and reckless investment decisions and it is not surprising that some of them end up losing their earlier wins in the process of making new contracts. Put yourself a ceiling that once you win say 10 trades, then you stop no matter.

In the same way of thinking, say to yourself that after losing a given number of trades, you stop whichever the case may be. This is because if, for instance, you say that you must win a given number of trades before quitting, you may end up losing a 100 trades without a single win. It is not a win or die competition.

The other way to think of this strategy is to put a ceiling that when you hit a certain percentage of losses then you stop immediately. In this way, you will not be limiting the number of trades you can participate in but timing your losses. If say, you discipline yourself that you will stop trading once your losses hit 30% of total trades played, then you will stop once this target is hit. You could have played 100 or only 10 trades before hitting the 30% mark but the bottom line is that it is time to hang your boots. The reason behind this is that people tend to run after their money by playing more games and in the process lose even much more. You have to be rational and objective and you should not let emotions that accompany your losses dig your investment grave while you are still alive.

Other investors also advise that you should put yourself a ceiling on the maximum trades you can play on any given day.

Choose your time frame

Time matters in this kind of trade perhaps more than in any other type of trade. If say, you are trading in the 60 seconds options, you need to determine your time frame before going into the real venture. You need to know when you are available to trade and when to close your shop. Selecting your time frame will depend on a variety of factors such as:

-Your type of trade. There are many binary options traders. Each trade will require a special time frame.

-How much time you have to oversee your investments and look for opportunities on a daily basis.

-Do you prefer a fast paced kind of investment that offers you quick rewards?

-Are your investments affected by certain economic events such as interest rates or new information in the corporate world?

These questions will have as many varied answers as the number of audience. The parameters of these factors must be defined before you get yourself in the trade. The process must be time bound if any financial gain is to be realized.

Select your best trading asset

This stems from the fact that you have to accurately determine the performance of this asset in the financial asset. You will only be able to do this if you have thorough knowledge of the asset. If what you know best is the stock market and you are able to perform a fundamental and technical analyses on the same, then it would best to concentrate and make bets in the stock market.

Many get into assets that they can barely explain their features regarding the market.

Each asset type has its own economic drivers that influence its performance in the security market. If you were trading in currency, for instance, you will need a thorough understanding of macroeconomics such as monetary policies as these factors have a direct bearing on this type of trade. My advice is that if you do not know about it, either leave it alone or invest in knowledge. You must understand the asset for you to make accurate predictions.

Level your risks

Each person prefers a certain level of risk. There are the risk lovers, medium risk takers and the risk averse types of investors. No matter your risk profile, you will agree with me that you should never bite more than you can chew. This strategy is meant to help you participate in binary trading only up to the extent you are willing to take the risk. It means therefore this strategy will strictly depend on your personal outlook and risk profile. I will classify the probable risk profiles into three categories so you can decide where you fall:

a) **Low risk strategy**

This strategy is meant for those who prefer low risks to high risks. This team does not wish to trade high risks with profits. While you will only enjoy low profits, you will also reduce your risks. If your risk profile falls under this category, then you can apply the following 'rules':

-Stop trading after 10 wins. Also stop trading after 4 losses.

-Immediately stop trading after incurring 8% losses.

-Stop trading trading if the winning ratio is 80% i.e. 20% losses and 80% wins.

-Stop trading after 10 trades.

It is essential you note that you cannot apply all the above 'rules' at once. If you are risk averse, you can pick either of the above to minimize your risks. If you decide to go by strategy 1, then you need to monitor the number of wins and losses as you trade.

b) Medium risk strategy

This is to help you if you are indifferent about taking risks. If you are this kind of investor, I recommend the following:

-Stop trading after 30 wins. Also stop after 10 losses!

-Stop the trade after losing 15% of trades.

-Stop it if your winning ratio falls below 75%.

-Stop the game after 50 trades.

Again whether you will go any strategy, it will mainly depend on your outlook. Just pick on any that suits the time.

c) High risk strategy

This is for you if you are a risk lover. Below are some important rules to follow:

-Stop after 100+ wins. No need to continue after 30 losses.

-Stop after 25% losses.

-Stop if your winning ratio drops to 65%.

-You can trade as many as you wish but ensure you are within the above mentioned limits.

The above are rules of thumb. Even though they are the most recommended, tested and tried, this does not prevent you from using your own figures. However, it is advisable that you operate within a reasonable range and the above suggested values are your best bet if you are to efficiently manage your money.

Technical analysis

In the earlier strategies, we made little reference as to how you can make accurate predictions as regards price movements. With many odds stack against you in the volatile market, it is worth learning how to predict future market movements. Technical and fundamental analyses are used by many investors to identify trends and predict future market behaviours.

Technical analysis is a method that uses charts developed from historical activities in the market to identify patterns and specific contexts where it is possible to predict future market characteristics based on the historical behaviours of the market.

This strategy of predicting the market future orientation is based on the belief that the market remembers and will likely behave the same way in the future as it did in the past.

If say, you are trading in the binary options with asset X and it is possible to get all the data regarding X for the past 1 year when this information is presented in graphic form, you will be able to identify a particular pattern of behaviour. This can enable you to predict the likely direction that X will move.

Technical analysis as a strategy will help you predict the future market orientation with most accuracy. I have not dag deep into how to draw financial graphs and charts as you can easily do this as long as you have the data. With technology today, you only need to feed this data in financial software and your computer will do the rest for you. Some brokers are also adding value to their clients by giving this information to their clients.

Technical analysis if used correctly and in combination with fundamental analysis (discussed below) will increase your profits because you will get your guess wrong. Sorry, I am not guaranteeing you a 100% probability of getting it right but I am assuring you a higher a chance getting it right. Why get it wrong any way?

Fundamental analysis

A discussion on investment strategies would not only be incomplete but perhaps null too without a discussion on fundamental analysis. This too as earlier mentioned is to help you predict the future market orientation. In binary trading, studying the 'fundamentals' of a particular asset is useful in predicting the future orientations of asset prices.

Fundamental analysis focusses majorly on economic factors and overall economic climate that has a direct bearing on the prices of the assets. These economic statistics can include interest rates, unemployment rates, inflation and national debt. A good example was the 2008 crisis that hit most economies and then was a good time to bet downwards in binary trade market.

If say, you notice a significant change in the interest rates from the financial information just released and your binary option is currencies, then it is possible to assess what effect the change in interest rates will have on exchange rates and thus you will make accurate decisions.

Most economic information are released in real time. Constantly monitoring new information will greatly help you increase your profits as you will find yourself ahead of the market. When combined together with technical analysis, I am certain you will be able to say with high reliability whether a security price will move up or down. It is time you start being sure!

Martingale betting

Martingale method of betting is perhaps one of the most interesting strategies I will tell you about in this book. The word interesting is perhaps an underestimation of the extent to which this method is funny.

Martingale is a method of betting that advocates that you increase the amount of investments after every loss suffered! The principle of martingale demands that you double your investments after every loss until a winning position is achieved.

For instance, if I had bet in the binary trade with an initial investment of $200 in binary options, losing this investment will invite you to bet again with another $200. If luck is not in your second bet and you lose another time, you will add your bet by

$400. This should go on until a winning closing position is achieved. This looks weird, doesn't it?

But what is the rationale? The advocates of this stratify base it on the premise that additional investments will offset the losses and you will achieve the level of profitability sought once you achieve a winning position. This is mathematically correct but in my own view, theoretically risky. If one suffers subsequent losses even after betting in many trades, the loss can only become large and by closing time, I believe nothing will be left in your trading account. In fact, you will be at the legal unit filing a suit against the inventors of this principle and its proponents. Even at the furthest stretch of your imagination, do not expect me to advice you to try this strategy but remember the choice is yours. I know the psychology of a trader is formatted such that it always wants to run after its money. This can only result into more losses. Even though there exists many books and websites extolling the merits of martingale (they are right anyway), I always advise investors to shun this strategy as it is equivalent to running after your money- something quite dangerous.

Key notes: What you need to know to succeed in binary options trading;

Binary options are easy to trade but it is not all that easy to make money with binary options. Whereas there are many people who will tell you that all you need to to do is to sign up for an account and start trading, binary options like other trades require more than just that. Life cannot be that easy. Before venturing into the market, equip yourself with the following:

-A thorough knowledge of the trade. I hope this book has provided you with adequate information on how best to invest in binary options.

-Sharpen your skills so that you can read and interpret data presented in whatever form of charts. This will aid you in technical analysis.

-Learn how to efficiently manage your capital. I always advise to only trade with the amount you are 'willing' to lose as well. Do not trade with borrowed money.

-Keep abreast with real time news about financial markets.

-Last but not ultimately the least, pick on a reputable broker. Not any Tom, Dick and Harry that poses as a broker is your best guess.

*Key point/action step

I leave the choice of the strategy you would like to apply to start reaping gains in the world of binary trading to you. Remember each strategy suits different individuals and works in different environments. However, whichever strategy you pick on, do not leave behind technical and fundamental analyses. The latter strategies can never be outdated. A combination of these strategies with proper capital management strategies yields the best profits. Also, I will be doing injustice to your investment dreams if I did not tell you how to identify scam in binary options. As a binary trader, you wish to ensure the safety of your investments but the world of binary options is full of uncouth investors who will want to milk out even your last dollar. The below can help you spot a scam in binary options:

*Unrealistic promises. If the deal seems to be too good, think twice. Money is hard to come by and any deal that offers you promises too high to be true is a scam. The financial market is full of skilled investors just like you and you should not expect to win all the time.

*A broker who promises wealth overnight is not a genuine one. You will meet some brokers who tell you that you will retire within just months after you begin trading. Hey! Wait a minute. Why are they in the business themselves. What makes you achieve highly in the options market is your hard work, dedication, discipline and winning strategies not empty promises.

So next time you meet any person posing as a binary options broker, be on the look for these indicators.

How to Apply What You've Learned?

In this book, we have not just demystified the world of binary options but also proved that binary options are for everyone. I believe that I started with risk averse investors but as they read this concluding chapter, they already know that binary trading is worth the risk. You learnt from this book that though the world of binary options present numerous opportunities to make wealth, there are also risks and other odds stack against you. The book, however, does not leave you with the burden of solving this dilemma on your own. It goes ahead to propose to you nine strategies that you can use to manage risks while maximizing returns. However, to find this guide helpful, you will need to apply the plethora of knowledge you have gained from this guide to the real market together with what you already know. These words of Robert Allen should be your pillar in every decision.

"How many millionaires do you know who have become wealthy by investing in a savings account? I rest my case."

- Robert Allen

I too rest my case here.